How to Analyze People

The Ultimate Guide to Using Psychological Techniques to Read People, Body Language, and Learn About the Human Psyche

Jonathan Wilkens

Table of Contents

© Copyright 2018 by Jonathan Wilkens - All rights reserved.

The following eBook is reproduced below with the goal of providing information that is as accurate and reliable as possible. Regardless, purchasing this eBook can be seen as consent to the fact that both the publisher and the author of this book are in no way experts on the topics discussed within and that any recommendations or suggestions that are made herein are for entertainment purposes only. Professionals should be consulted as needed prior to undertaking any of the action endorsed herein.

This declaration is deemed fair and valid by both the American Bar Association and the Committee of Publishers Association and is legally binding throughout the United States.

Furthermore, the transmission, duplication or reproduction of any of the following work including specific information will be considered an illegal act irrespective of if it is done electronically or in print. This extends to creating a secondary or tertiary copy of the work or a recorded copy and is only allowed with express written consent from the Publisher. All additional rights reserved.

The information in the following pages is broadly considered to be a truthful and accurate account of facts and as such any inattention, use or misuse of the information in question by the reader will render any resulting actions solely under their purview. There are no scenarios in which the publisher or the original author of this work can be in any fashion deemed liable for any hardship or damages that may befall them after undertaking information described herein.

Additionally, the information in the following pages is intended only for informational purposes and should thus be thought of as universal. As befitting its nature, it is presented without assurance regarding its prolonged validity or interim quality. Trademarks that are mentioned are done without written consent and can in no way be considered an endorsement from the trademark holder.

Introduction

Thank you so much for purchasing *How to Analyze People: The Ultimate Guide to Using Psychological Techniques to Read People, Body Language, and Learn about the Human Psyche!*

We all wish we were better at reading people in our everyday life, but rarely do people take the initiative to go out and learn these basic skills. So I congratulate you on taking that first step in acquiring these very useful people skills!

The human race, as you are well aware, is a very complex species. But thanks to advancements in technology, there are now more ways than ever to analyze people in your everyday life, from loved ones to strangers.

The following chapters will lead you to discover the reasons why learning these skills is vital to get ahead in life, teach you easy-to-use techniques to read body language, and much more! If one of your strong desires is to step into the shoes of other people, this is the fast-track way of fulfilling that desire!

As you make your way through this book, you will gain the knowledge about varying personality types that drive people, how humans communicate and interact with one another, how to use social and verbal cues to figure out what you need to know about others, and more! Honing the skill of analyzing others is more than just diving skin deep. It's about understanding the way we mentally function in everyday life.

There are plenty of books that discuss analyzing others on the market, so thanks again for choosing this one! Every effort was made to ensure it is full of as much useful information as possible. Please enjoy!

CHAPTER 1

<u>Benefits of Acquiring Analyzing Techniques</u>

We, as human beings, are wildly complex. There is much more to each individual than what is skin deep. We all endure our own unique experiences, have our own personalities, and have varying perspectives of the world we dwell in. This chapter outlines the benefits that are paired with taking the time to acquire analyzing skills!

<u>Ability to connect with others</u>

We have two different types of language: body and verbal. Over half of the things we say are not said at all, but rather shown through our body language. There has probably been at least a time or two that you wondered what was going through someone else's mind. Well, analyzing people gives you the capability to see deeper into what that person might be pondering over! This gives you the ability to connect yourself more firmly in their lives and understand their situations.

Ability to make long-lasting friendships and relationships

There will come a time that a loved one may need an analyzer like yourself to help them brainstorm, think of resolutions for issues, and help them through the entire thought process. As you can imagine, you can create wonderful relationships this way!

Analyzers are more considerate

Those who analyze notice the aspects of everyday life that many of us are blind to. This can easily aid in becoming more tolerant and caring of others. Pat yourself on the back if you have these qualities; they are sure hard to come by in today's world.

More reliable

When all of the above is put together, you unmistakably have a reliable individual. They dislike disappointing others. Analyzers ensure that they do everything in their power to make sure no stone goes unturned.

Highly intelligent

To be a fruitful analyzer, you must have the desire to tap into the human mind and learn why we function the way we do. As an analyzer, your brain expands via trying to understand a multitude of things that many of us often overlook.

Become prosperous

In the 'dog-eat-dog' world of business, having the skills to analyzer fellow employees as well as potential and returning customers can put you a major step ahead of other competitors. Learning to really understand body language can help you to notice signs during sales communications. If you take the time to notice the tiniest of non-verbal cues, it may save many sales deals with potential customers!

Prevent possible conflicts

There are other kinds of non-verbal cues and body language we utilize, both consciously and unconsciously when we are upset or angry about something. It is important to acquire the knowledge needed to recognize defensive body language and non-verbal angry cues. This assists in a variety of situations, especially in close-bonded relationships. You can scale back the anger if you take the time to perform the right steps of action when you realize a person is upset with you. You can prevent unnecessary conflict from escalating. This is a win-win, for you can put an end to fighting and negative commentary that will only end up tarnishing relationships.

Improve your self-presence

Learning analyzing techniques can help you become much more aware of your own body. Body language not only informs others what we are thinking and feeling, but it also influences how we feel overall as well. If you feel a bit down on yourself or about life in general, get up off the couch, stand tall and expand your chest. Performing this action just for a few minutes can help you regain that welcomed energy back into your body and mind, and create a feeling of self-confidence. Improving your own body language has an impact on positivity on yourself as well as those who are in your life!

Opens up opportunities

In the midst of body language, in just a mere half an hour, one person can transmit over 800 non-verbal signals to another person. By learning the ways of non-verbal communications, you can also teach your brain how to always know what to look for. In this, you may be surprised at what you actually begin seeing in the world that surrounds you. There have been many body language experts that have said learning the ways of non-verbal communication is like viewing the entirety of the world in high definition. You will inevitably be able to see a whole new layer of information that leads to a higher meaning of explanation.

Ability to see into social situations

Learning body language allows you to get a few steps ahead. While it teaches you how to read others, it also makes you privy to the ora you might be sending to others as well, leaving you to notice room for improvements. This goes for all types of social situations, even outside the workplace. The dating world is modernly vast thanks to technology and cellular applications. We can now meet people through device screens, which leads to more potential issues. The first time people meet, it can be naturally awkward. But you can avoid some of these feelings between you and the other person by becoming consciously aware of their cues as well as the way you are portraying yourself.

CHAPTER 2

Diving into the Human Mind

How We Perceive the World

Humans can be compared to living machines; we all gather information about the outside world, but we are all unique, which means we process and act on that information differently. Our brains work similar to that of computers, inputting truckloads of information in, processing it, and storing it in a plethora of ways, thus creating some sort of output. The core of the way we behave is due to stimuli that then produce responses; all while making connections inside our mind.

To have a reaction to the outside world, you must use one or all five of your sensory perceptions, also known as taste, touch, smell, hearing, and sight. These are responsible for feeding your brain with the right information to make appropriate decisions. You do not just see the world, smell the world, or hear what is going on, but your brain does too!

We stand out among the other living organisms in the world by our ability to sense the environment and then learn valuable intel from it and our experiences.

Feelings and Thoughts

Ah, human emotion. This is something that none of us can totally suppress, no matter how hard we try. This is one of the main reasons that receiving and providing feedback can be wildly challenging.

Back in the day, those who managed to survive constantly had their instincts, or emotional radars, on full blast. We used to have to trust our instincts for simple survival since we were susceptible to predators and other dangers. Fast forward to the world today, and instincts are still heavily prevalent, but in much different ways.

Many of us are taught to push back our emotions and instincts, especially when it comes to the business world. This is supposed to aid in business people utilizing their logical thoughts rather than acting on emotion along. But like I've mentioned before, you cannot totally hide emotion. This is why that despite the good news we hear, we often hear the not so great news the loudest.

These are just a couple examples of the exact reason why it can be difficult to read people. If you have folks in your personal and business life that are suppressing emotion, are you receiving the real version of them or a faulty one? This can greatly impact how we perceive and gather information about these people.

Habits

You can receive a lot of good intel from analyzing people from the way they act when they are the most comfortable. By observing their habits, one can distinguish many things. Habits are automatic actions we perform, which many times we do unconsciously.

Many actions throughout an average day go completely unremembered. But the smallest of behaviors tell us how we approach life.

Here are some intriguing ways to decipher people's personalities as you are in the process of analyzing them:

✓ **Habits That Reveal Personality**

<u>Shopping Habits</u>

⇒ Does one look at all the ingredients on nutritional labels?

⇒ Does one choose products quickly and without much thought?

<u>Toilet Paper</u>

⇒ Is the roll over? Signifies dominance.

⇒ Those that tuck the roll under are shown to be more submissive.

<u>Eating Habits</u>

⇒ Slow eaters like to remain in control and appreciate life more.

⇒ Fast consumers are goal-oriented, open to new things, and impatient.

⇒ Adventurous eaters like to expand the boundaries of their comfort zones

⇒ Picky eaters are neurotic in various aspects of life.

⇒ Those who need to keep food separate are detail oriented and very disciplined.

Emails

⇒ Take a closer look at your emails...

⇒ Those with lower emotional intelligence tend to use more negative words.

⇒ Narcissists tend to talk about themselves.

Punctuality

⇒ Those who are regularly late are more laid back.

⇒ Dreamers are overly optimistic.

⇒ A perfectionist cannot leave till everything is back in order.

⇒ The definer rebels against societal norms.

✓ **Habits of Genuine People**:

More often than not, people want to learn analyzing techniques to decipher if someone in their life is actually a genuine person. Here are a few tell-tale signs that those folks you are questions are indeed good people!

⇒ Speak their mind

⇒ Respond to internal expectations, not just external: What does this mean? It means that genuine folks spend quality amounts of time exploring their beliefs, expectations, and standards of life.

⇒ Forget their paths: Meaning, they are more authentic, not dwelling on what people think or think they should be doing.

⇒ Not afraid of failure: Genuine folks like to venture the road less traveled. They see failure as an important piece of the journey to becoming their authentic selves.

⇒ Able to admit when they fail: They are true to their feelings, even the ones that might be difficult to admit, like failure.

⇒ Don't judge: Genuine people realize that all people are on their own paths, experiences life is different ways. Instead of judging, they are accepting of the lives of others and encourage those around them to do their best.

⇒ Have great self-esteem: Genuine individuals can absorb conflicts, criticism, and failures well. They are accepting of others and their successes, and not threatened by it. They are solely confident in what their life consists of and what they are working towards/have to offer.

I know what you are probably thinking: Why in the *world* is all of this information in this particular chapter together? It's simple really. All of it is connected. From the way in which we see the world around us, how we feel, act and react to outside stimuli, and the way we present ourselves via our habits and personalities, it is all connected as a great, thorough way to determine the type of person those in your life are!

CHAPTER 3

Human Personality Types

There's a plethora of personality types that are seasoned through the human race, with these not even being all of them! While life experiences and lessons help create us into whom we are, for we are born hardwired with personality types that fuel the things we do and provide insight to our actions, speech, futures, etc. As an analyzer, I assure you that you will find this chapter not only intriguing but quite useful when it comes to acquiring the knowledge packed within the remaining chapters of this book. So let's dive in, shall we?

Personality Types

The Fulfiller

Veritable and peaceful, these individuals are interested in security and quiet living. To an awesome degree, they are serious, careful, and genuine. They are extremely inventive with regards to terms of core interest. By and large captivated by supporting and propelling traditions and establishments, these people are proficient and continuing on, working reliably towards perceived destinations. They would more be able to frequently than not complete any task once they have chosen to do it.

The Mechanically Inclined

Tranquil and held in nature, these individuals are fascinated by how and why things work. They tend to have amazing capacities with mechanical things. They are brave people who live for the event and are by and large propelled by and fit for extraordinary games. These people are much uncomplicated in their desires and are reliable to their partners and their inside regard structures. In any case, they are not unreasonably stressed over concerning laws and precepts if they hinder finishing something. Withdrawn and interpretive, they surpass desires at finding answers for rational issues.

The Kindred Nurturer

Peaceful, kind, and solid, anybody can depend on these individuals to get things finished in an opportune, productive, and finish way. These people are known to put the prerequisites of others over their own particular needs. Consistent and with sound judgment, they regard security and traditions. They have a rich inward universe of observations about people and, to an incredible degree, recognizing of other's feelings, at the same time being enlivened by the serving of others.

The Creative

Quiet, certified, unstable and kind, these individuals do their best not to conflict with others, and not at risk to do things which may create strife, making them unfaltering and tried and true. To an awesome degree, they are exceptionally innovative and elegant, which drives them to thankfulness for greatness. Not enthused about driving or controlling others, they are versatile and liberal and are regularly inclined to be novel and creative, which influences them to value the present minute.

The Guardian

Unpretentiously powerful, interesting, and sensitive, these people tend to stick to things until the point when the moment that they are done. Along these lines, they are natural to such an extent, to the point that they are stressed over their own particular conclusions the same amount of as they are about the sentiments, needs, and needs of others. They make confidence structures which they altogether stick to. They are outstanding for their steadiness in settling on the best decision, which makes them at risk to be individualistic, instead of driving or following.

The Visionary

Quiet, clever, and hopeful in nature, these individuals are enthused about serving humanity. They have entrenched frameworks of significant worth, which they live unequivocally by which makes them incredibly enduring, adaptable and laid-back unless an immovably held regard is undermined. Regularly competent writers, they are soundly rapid and prepared to see potential results, making them extremely enthusiastic about understanding and helping others.

The Analyst

Self-governing, special and descriptive in nature, these individuals have a remarkable ability to change hypotheses into solid designs of action. They are profoundly learned in making solid designs of activity, which abandons them to effectively get centrality from their fantasies and influences them to long-haul brains. They are known to have lifted necessities for their execution, and the execution of others. They are regular conceived pioneers, notwithstanding, will take after another if they know and can trust to tail them.

The Philosopher

Rational, one of a kind, imaginative geniuses, these individuals can end up being particularly energized by theories and considerations. Uncommonly capable and made a beeline for change hypotheses into clear understandings. They are gifted and reason, which influences them to quiet and held, which may make them difficult to wind up noticeably more familiar with well. They are individualistic, having no excitement for driving or following others.

The Get It Done

All around arranged, adaptable, action arranged, these individuals are "Experts" who are fixated on snappy results. They live for the very moment, which makes them brave people who live briskly paced lifestyles. Anxious with long elucidations, they put an awesome level of confidence in those they know and trust, yet not typically respectful of laws and fundamentals in case they block finishing things.

These people are awesome at building fantastic connections because of their relationship building abilities and capacities.

The Keeper

Practical, customary, and composed in nature, these individuals are inclined to be athletic. Not fascinated by speculation or thought unless they see the rational application, they have clear longs for the way things should be. Immovable and driving forward, they commonly get a kick out of the chance to be in charge. These people are generally great subjects who take extraordinary incentive in security and quiet living.

The Entertainer

These people are regularly masterminded and cheerful; they make things more diversion for others to their joy. Living for the event, they esteem new experiences. They despise speculation and nonexclusive examination. Roused by serving others, they are obligated to be the point of convergence of thought in social conditions. They have a decent advancement of sound judgment that makes them extremely down to earth individuals.

<u>The Governess</u>

Warm, surely understood, and principled these individuals tend to put the necessities of others to their own particular needs. They feel a strong familiarity with other's desires and commitments, making them exceedingly esteem customs and the estimation of security, which makes them interested in serving others. Need inspiring criticism to make a decent feeling of self-esteem, and they have a very much made feeling of usefulness and space.

<u>The Encourager</u>

Fiery, confident, and imaginative, these individuals are prepared to do almost anything that interests them. They occupy extraordinary relationship building capacities. They have an alluring need to live inside the methods for their inward esteems and are invigorated by new musings, be that as it may, depleted with purposes of intrigue. These individuals are receptive and ready to adjust well, with a wide extent of interests and abilities added to their repertoire.

The Contributor

Surely understood and sensitive, with astounding relationship building capacities, these individuals are quite often remotely connected with, with real stress for how others think and feel. They typically hate being isolated from every other person. They see everything from the human point and commonly loathe indifferent examination. Especially effective at supervising person's issues, and driving social event talks, they are propelled by serving others, and apparently put the necessities of others over their own specific needs.

The Ambitious

Creative, sharp, and rationally rapid, these individuals are awesome to a wide extent of things. They profoundly value debating issues. They get particularly excited about new contemplations and exercises, yet may slight the more standard parts of life. They tend to be direct and earnest and acknowledge people and are a remarkable stimulant organization. They are outfitted with the incredible ability to fathom thoughts and apply the method of reasoning to find courses of action.

The Managerial

Confident and real in life, these individuals are headed to be pioneers. They tend to have a mind-blowing ability to grasp troublesome definitive issues and make solid plans. Cunning and especially taught, they, when in doubt, surpass desires at open talking. They very esteem learning and obtaining new aptitudes, and generally, have little resistance to inefficiency or disruption.

Human Temperaments

While there is a wide assortment of identities that fit into a wide cluster of individuals, there are really only four types of dispositions that originate from the personalities you just read about. Where do these personalities come from precisely?

Amusingly, from humor. Silliness in this occurrence considers how our body liquids are available inside us. Every individual has somewhat extraordinary extents of these liquids than the following, and the power of one liquid over another definer our demeanor. The predominance of one's musings is expressed to influence the conduct and appearance of a man.

While the idea of the four dispositions hypothesis is ordinarily expelled by numerous in present-day pharmaceutical and brain research, it's intriguing to find out about and remember while examining human conduct.

Optimistic Personality Type

People with this identity sort have a tendency to be fiery, hopeful, light, and happy. They revere endeavor and have a high peril protection. Generally, Sanguine people are incredibly poor at persevering exhaustion and will search for more assortment and beguilement. Clearly, this quality may as a less than dependable rule unfavorably impact their nostalgic associations. Since this aura is slanted to please searching for rehearses, numerous people with this identity sort are likely going to fight with addictions. Their enduring wants may provoke reveling and weight issues. These people are outstandingly imaginative and may end up being mind-boggling masters. Additionally, they are marvelous entertainers and will ordinarily do well if they pick callings in a media outlet. They ordinarily have more characteristic capacities in the accompanying zones with regards to employment:

✓ Sports

✓ Cooking

✓ Fashion

✓ Travel

✓ Marketing

<u>Impassive Personality Type</u>

Some person with this identity sort has a tendency to be detached and is extroverts. They search for social agreeableness and comfortable associations. These people are devoted life accomplices and esteeming gatekeepers. They spare their relationship with old friends, difficult to reach relatives, and neighbors. People with this identity tend to sidestep conflicts and reliably endeavor to intercede between others to restore peace and friendliness. They are especially into philanthropy and helping other individuals. The perfect professions for those with apathetic identity are:

- Social administrations

- Child improvement

- Psychology

- Counseling

- Teaching

- Nursing

Irascible Personality Type

Some individual with this identity sort can be unadulterated and crabby yet is objective situated. People with this character are to a great degree astute, logical, and sensible. To an extraordinary degree rational and clear, these people aren't essential or awesome partners or particularly social. They abhor easygoing talk and acknowledge significant and essential exchanges. They would ideally be removed from every other person than in association of shallow, shallow people. Ideally, they have to put vitality in people who have tantamount master premiums. The perfect employment for the individuals who fall into the peevish identity sort are:

- Business

- Programming

- Engineering

- Statistics

- Technology

- Management

Wistful Personality Type

People with this identity sort love conventions and every little thing about them. Women cook for men; men open gateways for women. They treasure their families and partners and, not at all like bright identity, they don't look for peculiarity and endeavor. Honestly, they avoid it regardless. Some individual with this identity sort is most likely not going to marry a non-local or leave their nation for another country. They are greatly social and hope to add to the gathering. Being to an incredible degree consider and exact, these people are spectacular administrators of other individuals. The perfect vocation alternatives for those with melancholic identity are:

- Administration

- Social work

- Accounting

- Management

CHAPTER 4

How to Interpret Body Language

We spend our lives making sense of how to translate other people's nonverbal prompts. While we're made up for lost time with endeavoring to unwind their messages, they are furthermore endeavoring to unravel our own.

Non-verbal correspondence is actually the tongue of the body. You may deduce that you simply exhibit your emotions through your face; be that as it may, that is genuinely simply a hint of a greater challenge. Your entire body shares in the matter of either showing up or hiding your mental state. To control that show suggests you have to control your body's careless prompts. This guide will show to you how, starting beginning from the best.

Your Head

Your scalp can enlighten others to your mental and passionate perspective. Individuals have great and awful hair days, yet here and there that ought not to be ignored so effectively. When one is focused, maybe they neglect to brush out their dazzling locks. At a solitary look, one may pay heed that you may not be totally together right then and there. Or, on the other hand, having bed head may influence one to expect that you have a provocative night on the town the prior night. Regardless of the trim, style or shade of your hair, having a prepped appearance tells others that you are responsible for the way your day is turning out. On the off chance that you don't have hair, that issue might be tackled. However, it likewise leaves your foreheads to address. They can give away signs, for example, inordinate scowling which is a misrepresentation concerning how you may feel.

Facial Movements

Your other lasting highlights of your face can't be changed (unless you go under the blade and get plastic surgery!) however they can noticeably show and give away prompts concerning what you are encountering and experiencing to others. The littlest developments that our faces make can give away a great deal of what we are considering others. These are referred to by analysts as "smaller scale articulations." These are crucial in genuinely deciphering non-verbal communication since they can prompt a logical inconsistency of what somebody may state, which persuades that what is leaving somebody's mouth won't be as honest as it sounds. For instance, if you are pulled in to somebody and wish to awe them, you may include those butterflies inside you that you think you are concealing great. However, the smallest pulling of the muscles in such territories like the mouth demonstrates that you are freezing a bit within. Pause for a minute to scowl for a moment. Observe how your whole face feels when you do as such. There are numerous smaller scale articulations that individuals project outwardly when they are perplexed, lying, and so on. If you wish to be exploitative for good reasons, figure out how to control these slight expressions.

Eyes

Your eyes are like a spring of non-verbal correspondence. When figuring out how to speak with individuals all the more straightforwardly and altogether, you have to find out how to adjust your looking and gazing, for there is a scarcely discernible difference. An excessive amount of investigating another person's eyes can cause uneasiness in the other individual, while too little can influence you to appear to be uninterested. This incorporates eye motions, for example, eye rolls, and so on. A twinkle in the eye can influence others around you to feel calm, don't disparage the energy of a grin or grin!

Neck and Chin

Your chin and neck are not to be overlooked! While they are both facial highlights we are conceived with and can't change, on the off chance that you are continually sticking your jaw out before you, individuals may read you and accept you adamantly. The neck can be adaptable and isn't a settled territory of the body. Be that as it may, the way you hold your head up can say a great deal in regards to you as a man and furthermore what you may think or feeling at a specific time. If you hold your head straight up, you will seem sure. On the off chance that your eyes are continually examining the floor, the contrary will appear to be valid.

Your Middle

If you hold your neck up pleasant and straight, at that point, your middle will take after this activity and adjust ideal alongside it. Certainty will appear on the off chance that you hold your shoulders and back straight and not slouching forward. On the off chance that you rather list more around the middle, maybe you are attempting to pick up the consideration of somebody who is thoughtful. Incessant hanging in the middle zone tells others that you may not feel great physically or rationally or that you are extremely unconfident in yourself. Keeping yourself in a strong upright position has more great impacts than non-verbally advising individuals you are sure about yourself. Continually permitting your middle zone of the body to droop will prompt an assortment of bothersome medical issues later on. So sit up straight!

Arms and Hands

Your upper appendages offer an approach to maybe the most fundamental and most simple to peruse apparatuses of the human body with regards to precisely perusing forms of non-verbal communication dialects. They can non-verbally impart a ton of things, including things you wish not to educate others around you of. Intemperate hand squirming can depict weariness or tension. Firmly folding your arms may influence you to appear as though you are furious. Self-important quirks like putting your arms akimbo might be accidental, yet other individuals exceptionally read into those sorts of idiosyncrasies. It is essential on the off chance that you would prefer not to give yourself away from an excess of that you figure out how to impartially shield your hands and arms from giving endlessly impressions that are really not consistent with you. The most prescribed approach to keep your hands and arms is to hold them in your lap. When you are standing, keep them at your sides or in another resting place that is agreeable to you with the goal that it doesn't look compelled to other individuals.

Legs

The lower appendages of your body give away the same amount of as your furthest points do. On the off chance that you firmly fold your legs, this may make a "shut off" view to other individuals. Be that as it may, spreading them out influences you to appear to be excessively joyful and indiscreet. To make an agreeable, casual and receptive feel to others, you should be casual however less so it appears as though you are exhausted with the current circumstance. What we wear can make contrasts in this, notwithstanding. Clearly, ladies who wear skirts should keep their legs shut more tightly than if they are wearing jeans. This is the reason it is worried to not wear too shy of skirts or other dress that influences you to feel awkward in your own particular skin. The nervousness of attempting to look great in pieces of attire that you generally don't feel your best in will show to others.

On edge, sentiments can likewise introduce themselves physically through the methods for over the top leg shaking and foot tapping. Individuals who fall off nervous may simply need to consume off a couple of overabundance calories, yet more than likely they feel restless about the circumstance around them or about something that might be at the forefront of their thoughts. The legs make up the greatest piece of the human body, so even with the littlest developments, individuals pay heed. Rather than shaking your legs, be aware of different ways you can keep this. To enable the substantial butterflies, to make it a propensity, even in situations that aren't the most agreeable, to sit with your legs tenderly crossed and your hands pleasantly collapsed in your lap. Not exclusively will other individuals pay heed to how quiet you appear to be. However, it will help you to settle sentiments of nervousness too.

Feet

If you are somebody that shakes their legs, at that point you unavoidably will shake your feet at the same time too. There is likewise the tapping of toes, which can show to others that you may be in a surge or restless to go ahead. Tapping of the feet likewise might be utilized to pick up the consideration of someone else if you would prefer not to put on a show of being discourteous if you say something. Toe tapping is ordinarily a non-verbal communication that is utilized when somebody feels constrained for time and does not have any desire to take part in discussion inconsiderately, regardless of whether it would make history quicker. In any case, in all actuality, these individuals might be viewed as discourteous in any case or out and out irritating with all that tapping!

Did you realize that your feet can likewise convey to others of dreadful emotions and certainty? It is about the way you move from point A to point B. On the off chance that you stroll in a walk that is straight and solid, you appear to be somebody that individuals can rely upon. Great stance of any kind depicts certainty to others. Slumping and drooping, be that as it may, depict an absence of certainty or ever a dread of where you may go. You radiate signals unknowingly by being either frightful or positive about your goal.

Additionally, on the off chance that somebody needs or is keen on connecting with you, their feet will point appropriate towards you. If their feet are pointing far from you, their psyches are on another theme, and it is a sign they would either rather be elsewhere or possibly in a slight rush or have somewhere else to be at the time.

A Few Tricks in Reading Body Language

- **Crossing of legs and arms** – This activity depicts conceivable protection from your thoughts or the considerations of others. The arms and legs are physical blockades that recommend that they may not be very as open concerning what you are stating, regardless of whether they happen to have a grin of their face and appear to be very fascinated by what is regurgitating from your mouth. If somebody's arms and legs are crossed, it is an entirely telling sign that they are closed off from everything before them, rationally and inwardly. While it may not be deliberate, it is still extremely uncovering of the way they think and feel.

- **The crinkle-eyed smile** – When you see the grin of others, a grin can lie through anything. However, the radiance in the eye and the wrinkles a genuine grin makes around the eyes can't. Grins that are bona fide achieve as far as possible up to the eyes. Individuals regularly grin to shroud their emotions and considerations. So whenever you see somebody grin at you, don't take as much notice in their magnificent whites, yet rather the creases that are made by the grin at the edge of the eyes. On the off chance that they are non-existent, they are utilizing the grin as a shield to conceal something.

- **Duplicating particular areas of communication** – While this sounds like a tyke like amusement, the reflecting of non-verbal communication is the way we tend to security with individuals unwittingly. In social situations as you draw in, does that individual fold their legs when you do? Do they rooster their heads similarly you do while chatting with others? The replicating of non-verbal communication is really a sign that the discussion itself is going awesome and that the other individuals are by and large very responsive to what you are stating. This is valuable with regards to arranging, for it indicates you genuine evidence that the restricting party is thinking about your arrangement.

- **Posture** – Think about a man of energy in your life, regardless of whether in the work environment or somewhere else. Observe their stance. More than likely these people will stroll into a life with an erect stance, palms looking down and convey non-verbally with open motions. Stance is basic in giving a story to others about your life. Standing straight with shoulders back depicts a place of energy. While slumping depicts less power. Keeping up a not too bad stance advises others that you charge to be regarded and elevates engagement to others, regardless of whether you are a pioneer.

- **Dishonest Looks** – I am certain a large portion of you recall the expression of "look at me without flinching when I am addressing you." Growing up, we were shown that maintaining a strategic distance from eye to eye connection was an ideal indication of lying. In any case, that is normal learning, such a significant number of individuals mislead each other even while keeping up culminate eye to eye connection. That is the reason those that are being exploitative tend to overcompensate eye to eye connection, offering it to others to the point of inconvenience. Seven to ten seconds is the normal that individuals hold eye to eye connection for, longer when they are listening as opposed to talking. On the off chance that you come into contact with somebody whose eye to eye connection makes you awkward, particularly somebody who doesn't try to flicker, they are more than likely being exploitative with you.

- **Look at those temples** – There are a couple of principle feelings that our eyebrows depict: dread, stress, and astonishment. It is difficult to have cocked eyebrows and endeavoring to have an easygoing discussion. If you are looking at something that shouldn't make any eyebrows raise, something unique is going ahead around you or with that individual inside.

- **Gesturing extensively** – If you are addressing somebody and they are continually gesturing their head, this may flag that they are worried about your musings or they may question your capacity to finish something.

- **Clenching of the jaw** – Clenched jaws, fixing of the neck and wrinkled temples are all indications of stress. It doesn't make a difference what is originating from a man's mouth, if any of these signs are discernible, they are concealing their tension, stress, and inconvenience. Maybe a discussion is driving down a way of something they are not happy with talking about. They key here is to observe any bungles of what the individual is stating and after that what their non-verbal communication is letting you know.

Chapter 5

Read People as They Speak

Since you found out about some non-verbal communication and non-verbal prompts, the time has come to discuss and consider the things that we verbally say. The words individuals say can be an indication of their identities. Indeed, even single expressions said by another can enlighten others truckloads regarding their wants, individual needs and needs.

In any case, the essential piece of breaking down individuals through their verbal discourse is realizing what they might attempt to conceal and avoid whatever is left of the world. Every last thing that a man says has a tendency to uncover in any event something that makes up their identity. The activities, convictions, and considerations of people all make up the parts of our identity as individuals. Every one of the things individuals do or think can reveal heaps of data about their identity, and in addition what influences them to up mentally.

Significance of Reading into Words

Our impression of the world and different people is made through our worries of other individuals. For instance, "Hello, did you become shorter overnight?" appears like a joke, isn't that so? All things considered, in the setting said it most likely was, yet when you analyze basic expressions like this, there is a ton progressively that is really being said.

Despite the fact that the individual who expressed this joke was more than likely simply joking, it demonstrates that they may be awkward with their own physical stature. It isn't by the expression he imparted that gave away his worries about his stature, but instead that we were wearing an alternate kind of shoe when he said it to his mate.

This individual may likewise be tired of his appearance physically also and may even be bearing a low self-assurance on account of their weakness about their looks. While in this case there might be numerous other distinctive elements that play alongside why this expression was stated, this is only a little yet prime illustration that we ought to figure out how to peruse "in the middle of the lines" of what individuals are letting us know.

Concealing Insecurities

For this area, we might use an alternate illustration. Envision two individuals at the exercise center, lifting weights. They don't have any acquaintance with each other however are standing one next to the other while working out. A third individual comes in and says "You both are standing excessively near each other, fare thee well, so you don't get hurt!" The separation between the two lifting weights was not sufficiently shut to end down in an exercise center disaster, so the way that the third individual made a special effort to tell the two rec center goers this was because they saw the circumstance substantially more risky than it very.

This provides some insight into the identity sort of the third individual, more than likely they are somebody who stresses a great deal and their view of their general surroundings is then misrepresented by the likelihood of cynicism that spins around their mind a considerable measure of the time. That third individual more than likely winds up plainly frightful of significant issues that ever emerge in their life due to this over the top stressing.

The Words in Which We Speak Tell Others *Who* We Are

The littlest of things individuals say are pointers of their identity as a person. The things we say convey what we require and also instabilities and other secret identity we may have, regardless of whether they are not specifically imparted accordingly or if we had diverse expectations when we talk them.

Many individuals tell jokes every one of the circumstances without considering that the words they are retching from their mouths can uncover significantly more than they proposed concerning their actual identity. Anybody that is a decent analyzer will get on the littlest of verbal prompts to evaluate them.

Discovering Clues in Words

On the off chance that the eyes are the window to the soul, by then words are the entrance to the cerebrum. Words address considerations. To comprehend another person's insights is to tune in to the words that he or she talks or creates. Certain words reflect the behavioral characteristics of the person who talked or stayed in contact with them. These are known as word hints. Word pieces of information augment the probability of foreseeing the behavioral characteristics of individuals by examining the words they pick when they talk or compose. Word hints alone can't choose the characteristics of somebody's identity, yet they do give bits of information into the way of considering and behavioral qualities. Hypotheses can be made in perspective of word intimations and a short time later attempted by using additional information evoked from the individual or pariah affirmation.

The human personality is amazingly capable. When we think, we use just verbs and things. Descriptors, intensifiers, and diverse parts of discourse are incorporated in the midst of the difference in considerations into talked or created dialect. The words we incorporate mirror our personality and what we are thinking about.

All legitimate sentence structures use both an extremely and a thing. For instance, we should take a gander at this oversimplified sentence" "I strolled." Short and sweet, despite everything it comprises of the pronoun "I" and the verb the subject is doing, "strolled." Any different words put into this basic sentence are changes of the nature of the thing or the activity in which the thing is taking. Their adjustments are made purposely, which give analyzers insights with regards to the identity of the individual talking, and behavioral qualities of the speaker or author.

Word hints empower onlookers to make hypotheses or make trained deduces concerning the behavioral traits of others. For example, in the sentence "I quickly walked," the Word intimation "promptly" makes a sentiment desperation. Nonetheless, it didn't give the inspiration to the franticness. Somebody may "quickly stroll" since they may be late for a course of action or expects to be late for a plan. Upright people view themselves as tried and true and don't want to be late for plans.

People who should be on time tend to respect social norms and need to fulfill the wants of others. People with this behavioral trademark make incredible delegates since they would lean toward not to disappoint their managers. People "quickly walk" when they encounter general perils. A general threat may happen while walking around a dreadful neighborhood.

Advancing toward dreadful atmosphere could similarly show a hazard. Walking quickly to avoid an electrical tempest reduces the danger of a lightning strike or getting wet. People may incorporate "quickly" for a grouping of reasons; be that as it may, there is a specific clarification behind their choice.

Word pieces of information demonstrate a noninvasive technique to peruse people without their insight enough. The accompanying cases will indicate how word signs give bits of information into the behavioral properties of people when they talk or compose.

- "I won another honor." – The word piece of information "another" is an indication that the speaker of this sentence has won past honors. By letting it know in this way, they needed others to realize that they have no less than one other honor, generally knocking up their picture of self. They may want and need commendations from others to strengthen their confidence and general certainty.

Analyzers could consider this to be a weakness by the utilization of sweet talk and different remarks that could improve that person's self-image.

- "I strived to accomplish my objective." – The word piece of information "hard" depicts that the individual who said this expression esteems things that are hard to reach or accomplish. In saying this, it gives away that the objective they are talking about is harder than objectives that they normally endeavor to go up against. "Hard" additionally gives away that this individual put off the requirement for satisfaction and trusts that diligent work and devotion will end with incredible outcomes. Potential workers with these sorts of qualities would more than likely acknowledge challenges tossed their way with assurance and would be effective at finishing those undertakings.

- "I persistently sat through the address." – The word piece of information "calmly" can give away a few things. It could imply that the individual was very exhausted with the address itself. Possibly they needed to restore a telephone call that was essential at the time. Possibly they expected to utilize the restroom. Regardless of the thinking behind what this individual stated, they were clearly centered on something different other than the current address. Individuals who sit tight for a break before leaving to utilize the restroom cling to social standards. The individuals who get rings get and leave the room more than likely don't take after social limits too. Individuals who tolerate reliably by social limits can be viewed as awesome workers since they tend to regard specialist. Then again, the individuals who don't exactly stick to social limits are more qualified for employment that expect them to deduct in novel behavior.

- "I chose to purchase that model." – The word piece of information "chose" implies that the individual who said this sentence measured a couple of alternatives before making a buy. It demonstrates that they may have battled a bit with settling on an ultimate choice. This conduct demonstrates that this individual tends to think things through altogether before acting. "Chosen" additionally may demonstrate that this individual is typically not incautious in nature. One who is more incautious would presumably say something more along the lines of "I recently purchased that model." The word piece of information "just" recommends that this individual obtained the thing without much idea by any stretch of the imagination.

- "I made the best choice." – The word piece of information "right" gives away that the individual who said this sentence has battled with moral quandaries as of late or before and has conquered them. This attribute says that this individual has awesome quality with regards to their character and tends to settle on the correct choice.

Reading the Minds of People through Their Words

Repetition of Particular Words

"That car is powerful."
"This color is strong."
"I do not have the strength to study."

On the off chance that you are to take a gander at those three sentences above at first look, you most likely won't get many hints from them. In any case, analyzers figure out what to look like at the things individuals say somewhat nearer. Notice the words "control," "solid," and "quality." All of them mean capable. The appropriation of the words inside our psyches does not occur haphazardly, yet rather with the words we say are regularly in regards to our worries, wants, and needs. The individual who said the expressions above is worried about quality, control and being powerless. He likely needs to be solid, or he supposes he should be more grounded, or he may be worried about ending up intense.

<u>Narrating</u>

"I was walking around my two companions yesterday, and a major man showed up all of a sudden out of the blue. We as a whole idea he was coming towards us to start a ruckus, yet ultimately he turned away and strolled past us."

What is there to say in regards to this little story? It was really expressed by a similar individual from over that was worried about power. "Big man" is an impression of this current individual's want to be solid either candidly or physically.

Yet, any individual would have recounted the story a similar way, isn't that so? No. This individual expressed is this way, and despite the fact that the man left them, regardless he utilized the word pieces of information "huge man" in the sentence. This is clearly what he was worried about the most around then.

Jokes Hide Crucial Messages

'There are kids sitting at a table in an eatery. At the point when the server comes to take their request, one of the children says, "I will have anything that costs one million dollars!"'

Clearly, this child was clowning. Be that as it may, as you have adapted hitherto, there is a considerable measure of essential intimations with respect to that person in all that they say. This present children's worry with cash is really distinct in this joke. He more than likely has experienced childhood in a family with guardians that have shown them that cash is vital. Or, then again they may have endured monetarily because of poor assets, and so forth.

CHAPTER 6

Tips for Better Analyzing

The best piece of turning into an analyzer is that you don't need to go to a favor FBI school to get into the psyches of what individuals are considering and feeling. Individuals emit flags constantly; we simply are normally heedless to them unless we set aside the opportunity to wind up plainly instructed on the most modest of developments. It's tied in with recognizing what to search for to arrive at a decision about somebody and decipher their code.

- Begin with pattern perusing. This will help you to build up a man's little idiosyncrasies et cetera. A typical approach to do this is to give yourself an opportunity to watch a man's propensities. This takes persistence since a few people are truly difficult to peruse. Regardless of whether you think a propensity isn't important, note it in any case. When you glance back at your notes, even the little developments, propensities or different moves that individual made that appeared to be unessential at the time can pull numerous different notes you have scribbled down together.

- Did you realize that the topic of "how are you getting along today?" could be an inquiry that another person is utilizing to test you to translate your gauge? Sales representatives use this strategy often to peruse your standard and get your set up for a request that includes more inquiries to motivate you to buy something they are offering.

- Be mindful of irregularities in a man's benchmark identity versus signals, words, and activities that don't exactly fit in. This will enable you to shape a general identity to profile after some time.

- Ask particular, not obscure inquiries. Open-finished request doesn't work in really understanding anybody. Unclear inquiries offer a chance to meander for them to answer it, which makes it significantly harder to recognize any kind of untruthfulness. Make inquiries that expect individuals to give you a straight answer but don't be excessively meddling. Straightforwardly ask away, kick back and see without interference. This is the place you will find that you get your best inside data on this particular individual.

- As you have adapted, dependably be careful about a man's selection of words. They give an incredible understanding of what a man is extremely attempting to pass on.

- Pay consideration how a man inclines. If their middle is confronting far from you, this may show that this individual is feeling focused. It can likewise imply that they have considerably more at the forefront of their thoughts than what you are endeavoring to state to splash into their psyches.

- Gestures, such as rubbing of the palms, touching as well as rubbing the brow or rubbing palms against one's thigh exceedingly, demonstrate that this individual is feeling rather focused.

- Never think little of facial signals. Look for wrinkling of the temples, fixing of the neck and facial muscles, holding of the jaw and lip compressions. These are for the most part indications of uneasiness and misery.

- Watch how individuals tend to slow down. If you are watching and notice somebody that shuts their eyes longer than it takes for a basic squint, set aside the opportunity to make a sound as if to speak or puts forth to rehash inquiries or what you have verbalized, they are setting aside the opportunity to slow down to abstain from something.

- Excessive squinting, squirming and an absence of eye to eye connection are all indications that somebody is lying. Be that as it may, these can be forerunners to somebody who may feel on edge about a circumstance also. It is normal for those that are trying to pass off a flagrant deception to take a gander at those they talk with straight in the eyes. This can likewise imply that they are endeavoring to duplicity you.

- Other portrayals of somebody being untrustworthy are the use of dubiousness into a great degree illustrative organizations or a trembling voice.

- Especially in ladies, if you are to watch them touching the territory in the center frontal piece of their neck, this may mean they are "securing" themselves, which can be a flag of being awkward;

- On the opposite, men commonly will stroke their necks when in discomforting situations trying to bring down their heart rate.

- Eyes are not just a window into the spirit. Extreme squinting and the tightening of the students may imply that this individual might be troubled by what they are seeing.

- Utilization of cathartic breathes out, known as very capable of being heard and long breathes out, shows that a man is in outrageous enthusiastic pain. They will more than likely utilize visit developments too, for example, fast hand motions. These activities are normally observed just minutes just prior, and then afterward they have been found accomplishing something they shouldn't be.

- To enhance discovery of untruths, set aside the opportunity to watch youngsters and how they act when they tell a white lie. We as grown-ups regularly figure out white lies, yet youngsters still can't seem to take in this noticeable aptitude. They are awful at being untrustworthy, which gives those that are honing their starting examining abilities an extraordinary place to begin watching activities when lying. One must remember that a few grown-ups are greatly improved at lying than others. Those that are not all that great at it will give comparative hints to that of deceptive kids.

Conclusion

Congratulations! You have made it to the end of *How to Analyze People: The Ultimate Guide to Using Psychological Techniques to Read People, Body Language, and Learn About the Human Psyche.*

I hope that this book was able to provide you with the valuable insight you need to start reading and understanding those in your everyday life! We could all really use a crash course in human analyzing and learn awesome things about one another through the process!

The next step? To put the knowledge you have newly acquired to the test! Start with analyzing those that you know well and branch out from there! It may not be that easy at the beginning. So, practice, practice, practice! You can do so by analyzing those that are close to you – a relative, a close friend, or your spouse.

www.ingramcontent.com/pod-product-compliance
Lightning Source LLC
Chambersburg PA
CBHW050655250726
48662CB00002B/689